Debt Proofing Your Holidays: No More Juggle Bills

Escape From Debtors Prison Series

Rachelle & Tyrone Potts, C.P.A.

1

Debt Proofing Your Holidays: No More Juggle Bills
Escape From Debtors Prison Series

For information regarding presentations or products, call or write: Prosperity Outpouring To The Saints, International (POTTS, Intl.) Tyrone and Rachelle Potts (818) 501-1358
website: www.pottsinternational.com
e-mail: hisfavor@aol.com

ISBN: 0-9701780-5-0
Printed in the United States of America
Copyright 2007 by Rachelle and Tyrone Potts

El Shaddai Publishing
Post Office Box 13921
Torrance, CA 90503

Cover designed by Tyrone Potts

2

Contents

Acknowledgements

Introduction   7

1. Honesty Is the Best Policy   17

2. Change the Steps in the Family Dance 25

3. The Best Things in Life Are Free   31

4. Desperate Times Call for Desperate
   Measures   41

5. Where to Shop   45

6. When to Shop   53

7. Why Shop   61

8. How to Shop   69

9. Gifts That Keep on Giving   77

Epilogue   81

Acknowledgments

The ground work for this book was laid more than six years ago. From 2000-2001 we co-hosted an evening radio program called, Let's Talk Money, on KTYM, a local AM Christian radio station in Los Angeles. On a couple of programs we discussed debt proofing the holidays. In 2002 we actually recorded an audio tape on the subject in our corporate housing apartment bathroom while on the road! We were traveling extensively teaching financial workshops across the country during that time.

We took a hiatus from writing books for several years as we both pursued other business endeavors. In the fall of 2006 I received a word of knowledge from Apostle Joseph Prude confirming my writing gift. He also indicated through prophecy that the Lord was prompting me to once again take up my pen, as my writing gift would confirm the wisdom God had placed in me. I promptly informed my wife that it was time to get back to writing, so within days I began to use notes from our audio tape to start work on Debt Proofing Your Holidays: No More Juggle Bills.

4

Early in 2007, as my financial consulting practice moved into busy season, it became harder to find the time to dedicate to the writing process. I decided to put Debt Proofing Your Holidays on the shelf for the time being. Late spring I received yet another prophetic word concerning this book. The pastor indicated that it was imperative that I completed this book as soon as possible. The Lord wanted to use it as a precursor for this holiday season.

I would like to thank both of these men for their willingness to hear from God on my behalf. I will be forever grateful. Without the encouragement I received from them, it is highly unlikely that I would have found the determination to complete this book at this point in my life. My desire to do God's will in his perfect timing was the fuel that drove this project to completion.

Tyrone Potts

Introduction:

Early service had just ended at St. Peter Community Church and Maggie Kline dashed to her car. She hurried because she didn't want to fall behind schedule in her preparation of the largest family celebration of the year. On her way home she stopped at a nearby bakery to purchase danish for breakfast. Maggie thought a sweet snack would be ideal for mid-morning munching, while she focused her attention on cooking her Thanksgiving feast.

By noon the house was full of relatives and friends, some Maggie hadn't seen in months. Also, there were all sorts of wonderful aromas emanating from the kitchen. The smell of fresh roasted turkey, stuffing, candied yams, macaroni and cheese and hot apple cobbler drew the kids to Maggie's kitchen before she placed the finishing touches on the meal. But Maggie welcomed the company of the Kline munchkins; she let the children graze like cattle on the mixing bowls, pots, pans and cooking utensils she used to prepare her dishes along with the leftover danish she brought home from the bakery. Thank goodness she had the foresight to pick up those sweet treats. Somehow Maggie knew they would come in handy.

When the clock struck 1:00 p.m., the dining room table was set and everyone was seated around the table anxiously waiting to dig into Maggie's Thanksgiving dinner. Before they started eating, however, the Kline family had to fulfill their annual tradition. Each person recited a Bible scripture verse of significance and shared why he or she was thankful. Everyone gladly participated in the Kline family ritual and the Thanksgiving meal was as always the most festive and enjoyable time of the year. Nonetheless, there was one problem. The meal only lasted about forty-five minutes, then everyone's attention scattered in different directions. Uncle Fred and all of the men retired to the den where they watched football for the remainder of the day and most of the night. The youngsters went outside to play, while the teens went upstairs to the bedroom to listen to music and talk on the telephone. Pat and the other ladies sat in the living room to plan their strategy for Christmas shopping.

There's an annual competition between the Kline women. They raced to see who could buy the most gifts in the shortest amount of time at the best bargain prices. The Friday after Thanksgiving is crucial to the outcome of the race because it's the biggest shopping day of the year. The Kline women knew they had to make a good showing on "Frantic

Friday," so they sat and they compared gift lists and they strategized their attack of the stores.[1]

Julie decided that she would stand in line outside Toys R Us® at 4:30 a.m. after leaving the Macy's® "midnight madness" sale. Karla would grab some bargains at the Dillard's® white sale for grandma and Aunt Pearl, then snatch up the latest music CDs from Tower Records® for the teenagers. Pat intended to be stationed at central shopping mall all day long. She felt that she could maximize her time and buy more items at the largest mall in the county because it is replete with numerous toy stores, department stores and specialty shops. Once each game plan was set, the Kline women synchronized their watches, turned on their cell phones and pagers, and ran off like wild horses on the opening bell at the Kentucky Derby®.

Maggie always felt empty and a bit disenchanted after Thanksgiving dinner. She put so much time and energy into the gathering because she desired to make everything as perfect as possible. But, what took days, even weeks to materialize seemed to dissipate in a matter of minutes. Years ago, Maggie noticed that the shopkeepers no longer decorated

---

[1] The Friday after Thanksgiving is referred to in the retail industry as Black Friday. It is usually the largest shopping day of the year. Retailers expect to garner considerable profits that day. According to a ShopperTrak RCT research, in the U.S. Black Friday 2006 Sales rose approximately six percent (over the prior year same day) to roughly $8.96 billion.

their windows for Thanksgiving as they did when she was a girl. Now the storefronts go from pumpkins to poinsettias. No one seemed to bother much with Thanksgiving anymore, except her. Maggie started to wonder whether this celebration was worth all of the effort she placed into it, since little time was spent giving sincere thanks and appreciation. Worldly cares and desires overshadow this once treasured family holiday.

As Maggie sat alone at her dining room table feeling melancholy about the whole experience, God spoke to her. He said, "Maggie, do you feel used, taken for granted and unappreciated?" Maggie replied, "Yes Lord, I do. I work so hard and give so much of myself to my loved ones. It's a slap in the face to watch them respond as if they couldn't care less." Then the Lord said, "Well Maggie, join the club. Imagine what it feels like to be Me."

Immediately, Maggie started to realize that the emptiness she was left with after Thanksgiving dinner ended was miniscule compared to the Lord's unrequited love. She began to feel pretty silly about the attitude she developed regarding her family celebration once she pondered the long-suffering God experiences all of the time. He gave the world his only son, Jesus Christ. That was the greatest, most selfless gift of all time. People benefit from God's generosity and unconditional love everyday. Yet, many fail to appreciate, thank, or acknowledge him for it. They don't even honor him during the season especially set aside for doing so, Christmas.

Introduction

The more Maggie thought about the spoiled-rotten youth, the sports addicted men and the shop-a-holic women in her family, the sadder she felt. All the children cared about were toys and games. The teenagers wanted clothes and music, the men were more religious about praising their favorite football teams than they were about praising God and the women were the worst of all. They shop until they drop, buying gifts for everyone, except the one whose birthday they are "supposed" to be celebrating. The question is, 'If Jesus is the reason for the season, why do we go for broke every Christmas?'

Somehow, a make believe Santa Claus, with imaginary elves and flying reindeer has acquired more attention and reverence than the Christ, who made this holiday season possible. Had Jesus not come, we'd have absolutely nothing to celebrate. The affection of family and friends has been reduced to an exchange of overpriced merchandise from retail stores. It's as if we no longer know how to express our love for one another without buying items we cannot afford.

Although the Kline family is a group of characters we created to make a point, they are truly representative of a typical American family. Though the average American household has a credit card balance exceeding $7,000 before the holidays, we still begin to work up a spending frenzy right after Thanksgiving. We spend and spend and spend without any guidelines or restraints despite the fact that we are still paying for last year's holiday shopping spree. The year 2002 American Express Retail Index survey revealed that

the average shopper would spend approximately $1,700 on holiday shopping. For many, that number represents one month's salary or 170 hours of our time. This figure increases dramatically when we don't pay cash for our purchases because then, we are charged interest. It can take us years to pay for the merchandise and we pay four times the value (or more) of the items we bought. Unbelievable as this may sound to some, it is true.

In other words, you could be buying (considering interest charges) mom up to four bottles of designer perfume or maybe four ties for dad, though your parents only get to enjoy the one single item. You pay that much for a benefit they don't even receive.

Instead of singing Jingle Bells© we should be shouting Juggle Bills©, for our tune sounds a lot more like this:

> Juggle bills, Juggle bills
> Spending all the way
>
> No one knows where the money goes
> And we can't afford to pay   Ha!
>
> Dashing through the malls
> Is the game we love to play

Introduction

When the bill collectors call
We want to run away Ha ha ha!

When the doorbell rings
Oh boy we get up tight

And with the New Year brings
Big debts that are a fright! Oh!

Juggle bills, Juggle bills
Spending all the way

It 'st no joke
When folk are broke
It's enough to make you choke!

If you want your Yule Tide filled with cheer, the buck must stop here. Don't let Christmas leave you in the red.

The holiday season has always been my wife's favorite time of year. She can get caught up in all of the festivities: the caroling, the entertaining, the food and if she's not careful, even the shopping. Obviously she's not the only one. In fact, she's in good company. That's why this Debt Proofing Your Holidays topic is so important.

To many the idea of going through the holiday season without taking on debt sounds farfetched or even impossible. People childproof their homes all the time, so that little ones won't injure themselves

13

playing. But, how on earth do you debt proof your holidays? Debt proofing your holidays isn't very different from childproofing your home as both require exercising preventive maintenance in an effort to avoid disaster. The sad reality is that many people seriously injure themselves annually holiday shopping.

We have commercialized Christmas so much that we've lost its true meaning. Christ came that we might have life more abundantly. We have to be honest with ourselves. We reiterate, if Jesus is truly the reason for the season, then why do we go for broke every Christmas? That completely contradicts His reason for coming!

Many people don't know that the word *holiday* originated from the term *Holy Day*.[2] This is supposed to be a sacred time, a time when Christians honor Christ our Lord and Savior. Christmas is all about Jesus. It's not about us. Yet, we spend the season running ourselves ragged, concentrating on everything and everyone but the One who deserves our attention. Our pastor, Bishop Charles E. Blake of West Angeles Church of God in Christ gives a great example of a birthday party. The guest of honor observes many of his loved ones celebrating. However, when the time comes to open the gifts he sees everyone exchanging presents with one another, but no one brought him a gift. And it's

---

[2] See Dictionary.com for the origin of the word "holiday".

14

his birthday not everyone else's. At Christmas we are celebrating Jesus' birthday. He should be at the top of our gift list. Giving or doing something in his honor should be at the forefront of our thoughts.

We must be reminded that without Jesus, there would be no Christmas. December twenty-fifth would simply be one more winter day that passes by. He is the reason we celebrate the holiday (or at least He should be). We all benefit by making Christ the focus of our holiday season. For God so loved the world that he gave his only begotten son that whosoever believeth in him would not perish but have everlasting life. We can't beat God giving.

Chapter One

Honesty Is the Best Policy

...considering yourself lest you also be tempted. Gal. 6:1

Many of us want our Christmas celebration to please God. We've made it clear that debt proof*ing the holidays* is a way to help us do so and explained why it's necessary. But, most people have no idea how to debt proof their holidays. So our discussion should start here.

The process begins with being honest with yourself about where you are financially. It's time we obtain wisdom, not more bills. The second book of our Escape From Debtors Prison Series, *"Let My People Go!"*, stresses the importance of budgeting. In

Chapter 12, entitled, Your New Buddy, we provide guidance in developing an effective spending plan. If you don't know where your money is going, you will never achieve financial freedom. Therefore, planning for holiday shopping should be a part of your monthly and annual budget. We explain that the budget is a tool to help you meet your needs and achieve your goals. Maintaining a sound, spending plan lays the foundation for obtaining financial freedom. Budgeting also lays the foundation for debt proofing your holidays.

Making A List

We tell children to make gift lists, but how many adults take the time to make one? Apparently, very few! One of our mottos at Potts Intl. is: "Failing to plan means planning to fail." A retail association survey during the 1999 holiday season showed consumers spending 27% more than they had intended to for holiday gifts due by in large to **poor planning or no planning**. We should know whom we're buying for, how much we can afford to spend (on each person) and what type of gift we'd like to buy them.

In the process of establishing a budget for buying gifts, we mustn't forget the other expenses associated with celebrating. We call these the extras. These extra expenses include: cards, stamps, food, parties, decorations, travel and charitable donations because we should never forget God's house and those less fortunate when celebrating Jesus' birthday. Going through the process of creating a holiday budget can be a real eye opener. For most of us, the holidays represent limitless possibilities, but recognizing that we have limited resources should cause us to exercise some restraint.

Knowing When to Say When

As much as we would like to buy our loved ones and those close to us all these wonderful things, we must "know when to say when." If we are committed to debt proofing our holidays, we cannot give in to the pressure to give beyond our means. During her anti-drug campaign, former First Lady, Nancy Reagan, came up with the slogan: Just say no. We must "just say no" to all the commercials and marketing gimmicks designed to make us feel compelled to buy yet another gift! Shopping has become the drug of choice for many Americans. It's time that we as a corporate collective engage in rehabilitation.

Once we've been honest with ourselves about what

19

we can afford and what we can't afford, we must
then be honest with those on our gift list, as well as,
those who are not. Are we suggesting that you
eliminate people from your gift list? How could you
not buy Charlie and Trish a Christmas present?
They always have something under their tree for
you. This is the tough part. Preparing a realistic
holiday budget that doesn't require you to go into
debt often means making some sacrifices. It may
mean telling your spouse you couldn't afford the
gold watch she wanted, or your son he'll have to
wait until next year for the dirt bike. Because you
have to establish a cutoff point to your gift list, it
may also mean having to tell your co-worker,
neighbor or the mailman you just couldn't afford
the cookie tin this year. Being honest relieves a lot
of the self-imposed pressure.

Don't OVER Dec the Halls

We can't emphasize this enough. Don't forget the
extras. Your cut off point may also entail
streamlining party plans. Instead of throwing the big
blowout bash, you may have to limit your gathering
to a non-catered get together of only your
immediate family. Recall the Kline family per our
introduction. Maggie could have overextended

herself by having a catered affair and even inviting extended family and friends, but she showed self-restraint. What she lacked in the way of financial resources she made up for by willingly allocating additional time to the preparation process. Her homemade meal also adds a personal touch and shows that she cares enough to invest her precious time in the ones she loves.

Extravagant decoration plans may need streamlining as well. When you think about it, does your house have to look like a replica of the North Pole? The nativity scene on the front lawn and a reef on the front door should be sufficient. You don't have to compete with the neighbor's for the house with the brightest lights award, either. After all, it can cost a mint to keep them burning all night long. Let's not forget the countless hours it takes to hang and take down those lights, unless of course you pay someone else to do the dirty work. In which case, you are adding yet another expense to your budget.

Counting the Cost

The final phase of operation honesty, is keeping receipts for everything you buy. By doing so, you're able to compare your actual expenses to the amount you budgeted for gifts and other items. This holds you accountable. You must be true to yourself. Only you have the power to decide what your financial future is going to look like. The question is: Will you give in to the pressure to overspend and blow your budget right out of the water? Or will you rise to the occasion and take a stand to make this year the first year you don't go deeper in debt? The choice is yours.

Be encouraged. Even if you make the wrong decision this year, the New Year presents another opportunity to commit to not making the same mistakes again. You'll have an entire year to set yourself up for success. During this time you should be saving on a monthly basis in order to meet your holiday needs without going into debt. Keeping receipts for your records has another benefit. You never know when a gift may have to be returned or exchanged. In recent years, most major retailers began giving customers a "gift receipt" along with their original purchase receipt. That gift receipt doesn't list the price you paid for the merchandise. So you can actually stick this blank copy in the box with the gift and if the recipient should return or exchange the gift, he or she may do so without ever knowing exactly how much you paid for it.

Chapter 1 Exploratory Questions

1. Do you prepare a detailed shopping list (including spending limits) as a guide for holiday shopping?
2. Feel pressure to buy more gifts than are affordable?
3. Are your holiday meals/decorations nonexistent, modest or elaborate?
4. Is the thought of keeping track of holiday expenses difficult to bear?

Chapter Two

Change the Steps in the Family Dance

For whoever does the will of My Father in heaven is My brother and sister and mother. Matt. 12:50

We've made reference to self-imposed pressure and pressure from advertisements. You might ask are there any other types of pressure that you may need to relieve yourself of. There is indeed. Another type of pressure we must address extends from our families. We deal with 3 factors that lead us to over spend and incur debt in our book *"Let My People Go!"*. In Chapter 6 entitled, Guilty As Charged, we address those three factors: peer pressure, coping mechanisms and familiar background. But how do they relate to family pressure and debt proofing the holidays? Well, these three factors manifest themselves as family pressure when we draw the false conclusion that love comes with a price tag. Are we implying that some people out there still think they can buy love? We most definitely are.

Who Are the Jones'?

Here is an example. My mom's best friend's son buys her a $100 dress for Christmas. When she finds out, my mom expects me to do the same for her. Or the neighbor's son gets a $300 video game from his parents, so your son demands the same. In either case, our family member is crushed if his or her expectations are not met. This is peer pressure with a capital P; that's nothing more than trying to keep up with the Jones'. We have to stop for a moment and ask ourselves, who are the Jones' and why in the world do we care what they think? They're obviously trying to impress us! We should avoid getting caught in the trap of doing the same.

Coping Isn't Healing

Here's another example. You started a new job this year that requires you to work a great deal of overtime. As such, you haven't spent as much time with your wife and children. In turn, they begin to replace the quality time they are missing with you with a desire for more stuff. Overcome by feelings of guilt, shame and even fear, you give in to their desires and buy more things. Sound familiar? Hopefully you can see that shopping has become a major coping mechanism in this scenario. It never ceases to amaze me how people try to use purchase items like clothes, toys and whatever else to fill a void only a loving relationship can mend. Often we chose a short-term fix for a long-term problem. We do wrong things for all the right reasons thinking a band-aide® will heal the wound. No matter how well your intentions are, unfortunately making this mistake is bound to blow up in your face sooner or later.

The Hat Trick

Here is a final example. Most of us have grown accustomed to the family traditions we shared in when we were growing up. Well, regardless of whether these traditions are financially feasible or not, most of the time we cling to them as if our life depended on it. The Bible says tradition can make what's right useless, so to speak. Here we are focusing on our familiar background. Most of us don't even recognize how much it truly impacts us. Unlike my wife who has only two siblings, I have seven older brothers and sisters. We used to get together and buy gifts for everyone. But now that we're older, most are married and have children. I have nearly fifty nieces and nephews. We can't possibly afford to do things the way we did when there were less than 10 of us. We'd go broke!

So here's how we dealt with this source of family pressure. Some years ago we instituted the Kris Kringle method of gift exchange. So, everyone puts their name in a hat and selects one person's name? Instead of trying to buy gifts for the whole family, each person buys and receives one very nice gift. It's a wonderful concept. Of course, the parents have to buy the gifts for the names their children pulled. The Kris Kringle gift exchange is very affective, although it took us a while to get used to the idea. As a matter of fact, we still have a few renegades who buy more than one gift. Some of them are still experiencing money challenges on a regular basis because of their refusal to change and adopt a realistic financial game plan.

Can't Buy Me Love

I guess the moral of the story, when it comes to dealing with family pressure, is to understand that you cannot buy love. The value of or number of our gifts has nothing to do with how much we value the people in our lives. We mustn't make the mistake of trying to use external items to deal with matters of the heart. Love is an internal matter. Unless the real issues are uncovered and addressed, no amount of spending will ever be sufficient to heal the wounds caused by misunderstanding or lack of communication.

Chapter 2 Exploratory Questions

1. Do you overspend in an effort to keep up with the proverbial Jones'?
2. Do feelings of guilt, shame or fear dictate holiday spending habits?
3. As family size increases are adjustments made to gift giving plans?
4. Have you inappropriately placed a price tag on love?

Chapter Three

The Best Things in Life Are Free

...the gift by the grace of the one Man, Jesus Christ, abounded to many. Rom. 5:15

Now that we've established the fact that no amount of money can buy love (love is a free gift), we can't be remiss in expressing the fact that the best things in life are free. That's right, I said free. No batteries included. No money back guarantee. The best things in life are absolutely, unconditionally free. We all know air is free, and in some cases water is free. But you may be wondering what this has to do with debt proofing the holidays. A few years ago, we realized we could give untraditional gifts that cost us little or nothing, and those gifts have brought our loved ones more joy than any professionally wrapped department store purchase we've ever made. Hopefully that statement gets your attention.

Once we established a gift budget and planned to keep the holiday expenses down, God blessed us with some viable alternatives to our usual excess spending. We began to exercise our talents and got our creative juices flowing. It's consistent with one of our mottos: Think outside the box. Think outside the gift box, specifically. Once we open up our minds, we realize that we don't have to run to the store for retail items all the time because God has placed wonderful gifts inside each and every one of us and those gifts are to be shared generously with others.

Handmade from the Heart

I didn't win my wife's heart with a hefty bank account but with the sweet, loving stroke of a pen. I used poetry to express my love for her. My poems hold such a special place in her heart that she still has every poem I have ever written her. No one can put a price tag on that. Another example is our friend Dionne. She can sew clothes so beautifully. People actually think her outfits were purchased from Sax Fifth Avenue®. They are astonished when they find out they are her designer originals. Anybody can buy something pretty as long as they have enough money and/or credit to make the purchase. But, no one can deny the love and care that goes into handcrafting and tailoring something specifically for the one you love.

Then there are our two friends whom we have given the blue ribbon prize for their deserts. They can both bake like professionals. Phoebe makes a sweet potato pie that'll bring Betty Cocker® herself to shame. And Keeley, bakes a seven-up bunt cake that melts in your mouth. It costs her around $4.00 to make the cake and it's good enough to put the neighborhood bakery out of business. Homemade deserts make terrific holiday gifts because the main ingredient is love. It makes me hungry just writing about it!

Whether you can paint, draw, sew, write or cook, the options are endless. Maybe there is something else you can do that others would appreciate. Whatever 'your gift' may be, there is no better way to personalize a present than to make it. It just doesn't get any more special than that. People treasure your effort as a real testament of your love. Another good thing about making gifts is you don't have to go in debt to do it. We all have at least one special talent or skill, so making a gift is affordable.

It's a great way to debt proof your holidays because you don't blow your budget doing it.

Timely Gifts

Here's another untraditional gift giving practice we have acquired over the years. You may not be able to stuff it in a stocking, but your time and your services would be greatly appreciated by your loved ones. This one we experienced first hand. It happened several years ago when I was working two jobs and going to school. My life was so hectic I didn't have much spare time. One day my friend Mike came over to my house when I was taking a nap between jobs. While I slept, Mike washed and detailed my jeep. He vacuumed the inside, threw out the fast-food bags, waxed it, dressed the tires, he did everything.

As I hurried out of my door at top speed trying not to be late, I was stopped dead in my tracks. My jaw dropped to the ground. I couldn't believe it. My SUV was so dirty I had forgotten what color it was underneath. Now, I was looking at a vehicle so shiny I could see my reflection in the paint. On my windshield was a note left by Mike. It read, "Ty, I know how busy you've been, I just wanted to do my share to lighten your load."

Mike's self-less gesture touched my heart so much I never forgot it. To me that was love beyond measure, one of the best gifts I ever received. I could not stop talking about it. That did more than just make my day, it changed my whole outlook on life. Mike's generosity inspired us to do more for others. Now and then we take our nieces and nephews for the day and allow our siblings to have a stress-free, child-free, romantic time. And, I can't tell you how much they appreciate that.

It's amazing. People don't seem to think about doing things like that for others until extraordinary circumstance arise like illness or death. My mom always says, "Ty, give me my flowers while I can still smell them Baby." Our lives get out of hand on a daily basis. Baby sitting or detailing someone's car can mean the world to him or her. It would impact their lives so much more than an item you pick up at a department store sale. This manner of giving says to a loved one, "I truly care about you." And he or she will never forget it. Giving of your time and services is the same as giving yourself. This type of gift costs you nothing but love. It's true. The best things in life are free.

Keeping It Simple

Another time saving and money saving practice is

giving gift cards and travel miles (points) as holiday gifts. Many of us have already gotten into the habit of giving gift cards to those 'difficult to shop for' people on our list. This method works because you don't have to exceed your budget and the recipient has the luxury of picking out exactly what he wants. The travel point process is just as easy as the gift card process. Some of us gather frequent flyer miles from various airlines. Those points are the same as money. Once you accumulate a certain number of travel points you can purchase all sorts of items with your points. There are household gift items available, magazine subscriptions, hotel reservations, airline tickets, etc., many things your loved ones would greatly appreciate.

In other words, if you have enough frequent flyer miles in your account, you can buy a family member (or close friend) a plane ticket back home to see her Mom for the holidays using your accumulated miles. These days it's easier than ever to rack up frequent flyer miles. Some companies even have it setup where every time you use your credit card you accumulate more miles. But consider yourself warned not to charge just to get miles. Those cards typically have higher interest rates or require you to pay an annual fee, so you pay dearly to have the option of earning travel miles for purchases.

Everybody Does It

We can't possibly end this chapter without discussing the gift practice that many have done but nobody likes to talk about. It's the legendary "regifting" technique. Nearly a third of shoppers have regifted at least one or more times, according to the 2003 American Express Retail Index survey on holiday shopping. The first use of the term is attributed to the American comedian Jerry Seinfeld in a 1995 episode of his self-named TV show.

We need a working definition for this practice, so we'll start by explaining exactly what regifting means. Regifting is the skillful art of transferring ownership of a gift to an individual who is more likely to benefit from the gift. This process is to be taken seriously and performed tastefully and with the utmost tact. It is not to be performed for the sole purpose of unloading undesirables onto unsuspecting victims. In other words, we're not talking about that god-forsaken fruitcake that seems to be passed around year after year. That's a no-no. A good example of an acceptable regift is:

You received a lime green sweater from Aunt Mabel last year. However, it wasn't the right color to suit your taste nor was it the right size for you.

But when you gave it to your friend Jody, she loved it.

What we are talking about essentially is passing the gift on to someone who will appreciate and make better use of the item than you would. However, there are some rules we have to observe whenever we consider regifting an item.

Regifting Rules

1.   Do not regift within the same circle of acquaintances.

Wouldn't it be awful if Aunt Mable and Jody both lived in your city or town. The chances of Aunt Mabel dropping by while Jody was at your house wearing the lime green sweater would be too great to risk. Never take the chance of someone getting hurt by your actions. Regifting works best if the regifter is the only one who knows about it.

2. Only regift new items.

If you have used the gift, don't give it to someone else. That would be extremely tacky. Imagine if you had worn that lime green sweater and maybe even washed it a couple times. Jody might have even seen you wearing it. Then even though the sweater is two shades lighter than when you received it, you give it to her as a gift! That would be an insult to your friendship. She might decide never to speak to you again.

3. Never, ever, ever give the regift item back to the person who gave it to you.

This is quite possibly the most important regift rule there is. We recommend you form a gift tracking system by keeping copious records of who gave you what and whom you gave what. So you will know what not to give to whom. (Try to say that three times fast.) Simply put. You know very well that there are some people in your family who are clueless when it comes to picking gifts. To add insult to injury, they never give you a gift receipt. But because you love them you can't refuse to accept their feeble attempt at guessing your taste. You are better off planning in advance to pull a regift rather than sticking it in the closet to rot throughout all eternity.

Chapter 3 Exploratory Questions

1. What special talent do you possess that might be shared as a gift?
2. Who are three people that could benefit from a small gesture performed?
3. Do you earn points in any programs that can be transformed into free holiday gifts?
4. Is it possible to use the regifting strategy to help curtail holiday spending?

Chapter Four

Desperate Times Call for Desperate Measures

Greater love has no one than this, than to lay down one's life for his friends. John 15:13

Okay, once you've trimmed your gift list to a tolerable level, streamlined party plans and decorations to a minimum, adequately addressed family pressure and exhausted all creative free gift giving capabilities, what do you do if you still find yourself unable to get through the holiday season without going into debt? Many well-intentioned individuals find themselves in that predicament. If you find yourself in that boat, fear not and be of good cheer. You still have several options.

Bite the Bullet

Consider other areas of your life where you might be able to cut back on expenses temporarily to finance your holiday spending. It's a bit of a sacrifice, but it's for a good cause. Maybe you can go to the beauty shop once a month instead of twice for a couple of months. If you are feeling extremely brave, you might cut out the beauty shop for the month and be your own beautician. You can forgo guys night out for a few weeks and sweat it out in the kitchen yourself. And cutting your own grass during winter can be a great source of getting in more exercise. These are great ways to save a few extra dollars for the holidays.

In addition to spending less, you might consider ways to earn more. For example, some of us receive a bonus each year for the holidays. Instead of spending it all on ourselves (like we usually do), we could use at least some of that money to help debt proof our holidays. Also, some of us have the option to work overtime. Especially those who work in retail stores. And even if you don't work in retail, several of the retail stores hire temporary employees to help with the holiday season rush.

Retailers are not the only ones who hire temps

during the holidays. Several other businesses hire seasonal help including: the post office along with other package delivery services, candy stores and florists. These are all excellent opportunities for helping debt proof the holidays by earning more. Some of these places even give temporary employees discounts on items they purchase, which is another great benefit to help cut holiday costs.

Home Base

You might ask, what if the idea of spending more time away from home working is not very appealing. After all, that would pull people away from there loved ones even more. There are ways to raise cash without ever leaving your home. If you have the gift of gab there is telemarketing. All you need is a telephone and you're in business. Some telemarketers are paid by the hour and others are paid commissions based on dollar amount or number of sales. And if you want to do something that would allow the entire family to chip in to help, there's envelope stuffing. Some companies pay individuals to place there marketing materials in envelopes. It is not very difficult to do this either. Another option that is not as time consuming is the ever-popular garage sale. We have all probably had a few of those in our day. Garage sales can actually be fun. You can get the entire family to pitch in. In addition to raising money, you benefit by cleaning your home without it really seeming like work. Finally, you can use the fact that you get to go shopping when you're finished as a little incentive.

Chapter 4 Exploratory Questions

1. What convenience are you willing to temporarily sacrifice in order to help debt proof your holiday?
2. Could a part-time/temporary job help finance holiday spending plans?
3. Will you make a concerted effort to rally family support to reduce the cost of holiday celebration?

Chapter Five

Where to Shop

...seek, and you will find; Lk. 11:9

We've covered the basics of what debt proofing the holidays is all about. Now it's time to get into some of the specifics. There is an endless array of choices for the holiday shopper. Unfortunately, not all of the options are helpful to the goal of debt proofing the holidays. The prudent shopper selects wisely from the multitude of alternatives.

In recent history, the shopping mall has come to play an important role in the economic and social fabric of this country. According to the National Research Bureau, the number of shopping centers has increased from approximately 10,000 in 1970 to nearly 49,000 in 2005. On average in 2005, some 191 million adult Americans (U.S.A.) visited shopping centers each month.[3]   This represents close to 65% of our population.   United States Commerce Department statistics say these shoppers spent roughly $2.12 trillion!   So is the shopping center where you should begin your shopping odyssey? Together we will explore various options.

Let's Go Surfin' Now

The internet has placed the world at our fingertips. We're able to boldly go where no man could go a little more than a decade ago. Shopping on-line offers many benefits, one of which is it saves you money. There are several websites that actually allow you to bid on items you'd like to purchase. You can save 50% or more off retail prices in some cases. We've used the internet to rent hotel rooms, rent cars, purchase airline tickets, buy computers, CD's and books.[4] Shopping on the world-wide-web also allows you to comparison shop from the comfort and privacy of your own home. Once you've identified the best price, for the right

---

[3] Copyright, 2006, International Council of Shopping Centers, Inc., New York, New York. Published in *Scope USA*, dated 2006. Reprinted with permission.
[4] Nielsen/NetRatings reported that 19.2 million Americans surfed more than 120 e-tailers online in 2006 as of Black Friday. The equivalent to Black Friday for internet shoppers is Cyber Monday, the Monday after Thanks Giving.

merchandise, you can have the goods delivered right to your front door often within a few days.

Although shopping on-line offers the benefits of saving time and money, as well as, its convenience, many are still a little leery about the safety of internet shopping. However, there are several things shoppers can do to provide a secure shopping experience on-line. First, you must be certain to use a secure browser. Websites that use encryption scramble the purchase information you send over the web to ensure your privacy and security. Also, it is important to keep your password private. You should never share your password with anyone else, or else someone could use your password to make purchases without you knowing it. It's best to either memorize your password or at least keep a copy of it in a safe place.

Since internet shopping usually requires payment upfront, you must ask yourself if it is a good idea to pay by credit or charge card. The answer should be, only if you know you will be able to pay the entire bill when it arrives. Remember, we don't want to go further into debt. There are several benefits offered to using these cards. The Fair Credit Billing Act will protect your transactions by allowing you to dispute charges and withhold payment while charges are investigated. It will also limit your liability to $50 in the event of any unauthorized charges. Debit cards aren't required to offer this protection (although some may offer it).

Here's another important point, you should always keep a record of your transactions. Internet shoppers should always print a copy of the purchase order and/or confirmation number. They provide proof that you made the transaction. Keeping these things in mind should make you feel more comfortable about shopping on-line.

A Penny Saved

Earlier we mentioned the convenience of shopping without leaving your home. Shopping on-line is often stress-free and can be a wonderful time saver. There's no street traffic, no fighting for parking spaces, no crowded malls and no hassling with the children. But what if you enjoy being out among the huddled masses? Some people like window-shopping and all the other excitement that accompanies this great treasure hunt.

Discount stores, our next option, maybe the place for you. Places like WalMart®, KMart® and Target® may be your cup of tea. Usually, they have better prices than the retail stores in the mall and offer a wide range of merchandise all under one roof. So there's no need for gallivanting from store to store. You could potentially get all of your shopping done in one location, whether you are looking for household items, appliances, electronics, clothes, gift wrapping or other seasonal supplies and yes even food.

If it sounds like discount stores are your "one-stop shop" it's because they are. Most people appreciate the fact that there are items for every member of the family, from grandparents to babies and they have many checkout counters. Also, since these store chains are the largest in the world they have some of the best prices! They compete for the business of a price sensitive consumer, so they are constantly looking for ways to lower prices to earn our business.

But what if you're a shopper who wants the best of both worlds? For instance, if you want the quality associated with name brand products, but you don't want to pay a fortune. What options if any do you have? If you want name brand items at discount prices, then an outlet store may be just the place for you. We have actually been to several outlet stores and found some real bargains on things like: leather jackets, jeans and sneakers. They have a wide selection of items to choose from.

But if you are looking for something other than clothes like furniture, a TV or appliances, then you might consider wholesalers or liquidation sales. Wholesalers are businesses that manufacture goods for sell directly to the public. By cutting retail stores (the middle man) out of the process, they are able to offer the consumer great prices. Also, companies that are going out of business often have huge sales, because they need to liquidate (get rid of) their inventory. Although both of these offer the consumer opportunities to find bargains and reap tremendous savings, the consumer should make certain to examine the items purchased before leaving the store. They often sell goods "as is." This means the consumer may not exchange or return damaged items or items that are not properly functioning. In other words, what you see is what you get. So, find out what type of warranty if any is given. No one wants to take home a lemon from his bargain hunt.

When All Else Fails

Hopefully, once you have exhausted your on-line, discount stores, outlets, wholesalers and liquidators options you will have conquered your holiday shopping list. If you find yourself in the extreme case where you have not been able to address your entire streamlined shopping list via these avenues, only as a last resort should you venture out into department stores. We not so affectionately refer to these as the Retail Jungle. Even though department stores often tout their "deep discounts," the Retail Jungle shopper must vigilantly adhere to the old adage "caveat emptor," which is Latin for let the buyer beware. Like the mirrors in the Funny House at the County Fair, things in the Retail Jungle aren't always what they seem.

Often retailers have sufficiently marked up the original price of an item to more than compensate for a price mark down. In other words, just because they marked the price down 10, 20 or even 30%, doesn't automatically mean you are getting the best price on something. In addition, you must consider the old "Bait and switch" routine. Retailers may advertise one item at a deep discount just to get people into their stores. Once the unsuspecting consumer enters the store he is informed that while that item is available it isn't the best buy for their money, or there is a much better quality product for a slightly higher price (of course). So to play it safe, before entering the Retail Jungle, know exactly what you are looking for and what a fair price for the item is. Don't deviate from the plan by buying other things you did not enter the department store to get. Stay focused on your goal-debt proofing your holiday.

Chapter 5 Exploratory Questions

1. Have you used internet shopping as an alternative to traditional holiday shopping options?
2. Are you open to shopping at discount, outlet or wholesale stores?
3. Are retail stores the most cost effective place to shop?

Chapter Six

When to Shop

*To everything there is a season, a
time for every purpose under
heaven.* Eccl. 3:1

If where to shop has never been your challenge but
when to shop is your hurdle, then this chapter
should help you see the light at the end of your
holiday shopping tunnel. Answering the when
question is a bit more complex than it may appear at
first blush. The savvy shopper must consider the
various facets of timing his shopping endeavors.
Here we offer some helpful hints in this area.

Seize the Day

Since we're concerned with debt proofing the holidays, the sooner you get started the better. If you want to set yourself up for success, remember procrastination is your worst enemy. An old friend of ours used to say, "When dining out with a group, the last one to leave gets stuck with the check." Has this ever happened to you? The sooner you get started, the more time you'll have, a greater selection is available and you'll get the best prices.

You may wonder if there is such a thing as starting too soon. No, as a matter of fact, we suggest getting started on December 26th, especially for specialty items like wrapping paper, cards and decorations. You can save a small fortune and just keep the stuff in the closet, garage or attic until next year. Often you will notice sales for 50-75% off the day after Christmas. This alone could work wonders for your holiday budget. For a long time we never took advantage of these opportunities. It was too soon after the holidays to even think about shopping again. Now we are much wiser. We know the early bird catches the worm and the late one pays the price. A higher price as a matter of fact.

Off Peak Performance

Another great time to shop is during the off peak season, particularly during the late winter and early spring months when retailers are trying to move Winter clothes lines out to make room for Summer wear. They are willing to offer considerable discounts to reduce their inventory. You guessed it, that's another chance to catch some great sales. It may seem a little awkward at first, buying winter clothes in the heart of spring. But who really cares what other people think.

Remember, we already dealt with keeping up with the Jones' (See Chapter 2). So you've got the idea. We must stay focused on our game plan. Who knows others may decide to join you, once they catch the vision. It can be a lot of fun. Some of our wealthiest friends have been using these strategies for years. That's probably part of the reason they became wealthy in the first place. The wealthy are usually pennywise, so they don't end up pound-foolish.

We also benefit from starting early because it gives us ample time to shop. There's nothing like being able to stroll through a store knowing you are not in a hurry. You have more time to think clearly, because you are not working against a near deadline. So you are less likely to make rash decisions. Can you recall times where you have made last minute purchases in a moment of haste that you later regretted? As a result, you had to make a second trip just to return or exchange the gifts. If you've, "Been there and done that," make plans in order not to make that mistake anymore. Early shopping is stress free shopping. Stress free shopping is wise shopping.

Timing Is Everything

Next, let's tackle the best time of day to shop. In our experience, the middle of the day on the weekend is probably the worst time to shop. From the moment you pull into the parking lot, the challenge begins. Driving up and down the isles hoping and praying you will find a decent spot is the beginning of what you know is going to be anything but a pleasant shopping escapade.

The odyssey continues as you find yourself in the midst of the crowd. Negotiating through a sea of shoppers, you may feel like a fish trying to swim up stream. And whether it's your children or someone else's, keeping them under control multiplies the difficulty factor. A dozen, "Pardon me's," another dozen, "Excuse me's," and you just may find a couple of the items you intended to purchase. After you've managed to weather this storm, then you must face the "hurry up and wait" game.

Your final assignment should you chose to accept it is the long, long wait in line. This phase separates those truly committed to the process from the faint of heart. As you switch lines for the third time, you wonder why is whatever line you are standing in the one moving at a snails pace. Once you get to the counter and pay for your purchases, you smile as if you had just won the lottery and breathe a sigh of relief. But maybe you should wait to exhale.

The entire ordeal has caused some temporary impairment to your short-term memory. Are you on the correct level? If so, is this the correct side of the building? Which door did you come in? So where exactly did you leave your car? That is the $64,000 question. Tired of looking, you just begin to press the alarm button on your key ring hoping that it chirps soon. Then you can forget the whole ordeal. Does this little tale sound familiar? If so, maybe you should volunteer to be the president of your local chapter of BSA. Battered Shoppers Anonymous is the support group for those who have been wounded in their tour of holiday shopping duty.

Since fewer people work on the weekends, that's the time they tackle the chore of holiday shopping. To make your shopping experience more efficient and effective, you must think of it as a game of chess. To avoid the turbulent waters, you have to stay a step ahead of your competition. It may not be the best fit for your schedule, but shopping on weekdays up until early afternoon before others usually get off work, is an excellent time. Then there's early morning on the weekends. Making the sacrifice of adjusting your schedule should prove to be fruitful.

During weekdays and early weekend hours you shouldn't have any problem finding a parking space. Having the pick of the litter where parking is concerned may even make you feel like employee of the month. This royal treatment does wonders for your disposition as you start your shopping excursion off on the right foot. Also, foot traffic is rather low and lines are much shorter. This will reduce the amount of time you spend wading through people and standing in line. Finally, fewer cars in the parking lot mean less guesswork when you are looking for your car on the way out too!

Drama Free

Can stress impact the quality of our decision-making? Does our emotional state affect our purchasing choices? The answer to both of these questions is a resounding yes. In the Off Peak

When to Shop

Performance and Timing Is Everything sections of this chapter we provided the formula for eliminating (or at least minimizing) the stress associated with shopping when stores are crowded (simply put, don't do it). This is one of the major external factors impacting our shopping experience and often a hindrance to debt proofing our holidays. Now let's turn our attention to internal factors that represent debt proofing your holiday roadblocks.

Your emotional state does affect how you shop. Shopping while anxious, sad, depressed or angry can have a negative impact on purchase decisions. Our judgment gets clouded by concerns and perhaps even the chemical balances of our bodies. So when we are experiencing these types of emotions or sensations, it probably is not the best time to shop. The difficulty lies in recognizing the onset of these "moods" and making the quality decision to put the brakes on your shopping plans until they subside.

Negative emotional states are not the only culprits. Surprisingly, feeling euphoric can have the same undesirable affect. When you're too excited or overjoyed there's a tendency to go overboard. Intoxicated by whatever turn-of-events gave rise to this emotional state, a shopper in this mind frame is less inhibited. He's more likely to behave in a carefree manner that amounts to exercising poor judgment. Just like it's unsafe to drive while drunk, getting behind the wheel of a shopping cart while emotionally charged is a recipe for disaster too! If

59

we had it our way, shopping in this condition would be illegal as well.

We suggest shopping when you feel even-tempered. A calm, cool and collected shopper generally makes better purchase decisions. Never shop in an effort to medicate when you are feeling emotionally unstable. Decisions made in the "heat of the moment," may lead to buyer's remorse, wasted time returning purchases and wasted money if the store where the item was bought has a no refund policy. It may become habit forming, and it's certainly not conducive to debt proofing your holidays.

Chapter 6 Exploratory Questions

1. Is the thought of beginning shopping the day after Christmas hard to digest?
2. Do you tend to procrastinate when it comes to holiday shopping?
3. Would changing shopping days/times make the process less stressful?
4. Is emotional spending an area of concern?

Chapter Seven

Why Shop

For in pouring this fragrant oil on My body, she did it for My burial. Matt. 26:7

Christmas has become such an integral part of our society that most of us never stop to consider why we buy presents. We have established family traditions which are activated like autopilot. Much like the Kline family in our introduction, at some point in late November, subconsciously we shift into holiday mode. If we were to ask the average person why they shop (buy holiday gifts), we'd probably get a response like, "In order to express my love to the people I care about," or, "Because they always give me a gift." In this chapter we will address these motives for giving.

The Spoils of War

In the last chapter I mentioned the fact that people try to medicate themselves with shopping. We should always shop with a specific purpose in mind, not just because it makes us feel good. Shopping has reached epidemic proportions in a society where people boldly characterize themselves as shop-a-holics and Name-Brand junkies for all of the wrong reasons. We are living in a day and age where bratty behavior is looked upon in a favorable light. Everything that used to be right side up is now up side down. Now-a-days people sport license plate frames, shirts and baseball caps that read: Spoiled Rotten, as if that's something of which they are proud.

Webster's dictionary defines a brat as an ill mannered, annoying child. And we all know what spoiled rotten means. When a piece of meat sits out too long it spoils and becomes so rancid that all you can do is place it in the garbage. Likewise, if you have ever bitten into a rotten piece of fruit you've learned that there is nothing pleasant about that experience. The first thing you probably did was spit it out of your mouth. These are well known facts and they should tell us that being spoiled rotten is not a good thing. When something is spoiled rotten you can't use it. It must be thrown away.

God does not spoil us. We could all take some wonderful parenting lessons from Him. We are His children but He doesn't give us everything we want. The scripture says He supplies all our need- our needs, not our wants. God does grant us some of our desires, the ones that line up with His will for us. But He doesn't always deliver them within the time frame we want them. God doesn't spoil us rotten because He knows that He wouldn't be able to use us if He did. We say we want to be used mightily of God. But, do we really want to be used or do we just want what we want? God is a good parent. He is not about to make us spoiled brats.

On the other hand, let's talk about how the typical parent spoils his children. Whatever they see, they want and whatever they want, they get. Many children have become spoiled rotten brats thanks to their parents. Ouch! I wish we didn't have to go there. But we'd be remised if we didn't. It would be ridiculous to discuss 'why we shop' and not adequately deal with this issue. So forgive me if I step on some toes, as it's time for a reality check.

In all honesty I believe that most parents, buy and buy and buy because they love their children. They want their children to have all of the things they didn't have when they were growing up. They want to make their children happy. The problem is:

whether your intentions are good or not, you are setting your child up to fail. Here's the real deal: You have them live this wonderful, whimsical, fairy-tale existence until they turn 18. Then, when they become young adults, they are faced with the rude awakening that life is not a trip to Disney Land®. You don't have any money to pay for their college education because you spent it all on toys and clothes and meaningless junk. How do you tell your child that his college fund is hanging in his closet?

Your children learn the hard way that things are not given to them on a silver platter. Instead they have to work hard for everything they get. Often times the harsh realities of life deal your children so many blows they decide they don't want to face the fire anymore. So they run back home to you, their loving parent, where they remain indefinitely. Or, they just continue to drain money from you on a consistent basis. Congratulations. You just created a financial out care patient.

Are they happy then? No! Are you happy? Of course not! The child you love has become an irresponsible adult and you helped facilitate the process. You know that you are a good parent, when and only when, your child is independent enough to stand on his or her own two feet by taking care of themselves without your financial support. Many of us who claim to be good parents just aren't. One of our relatives used to say: "Just because your mouth says it don't make it real."

Life is no bed of roses. And even if it were, all roses have thorns. So what if everything wasn't peachy when you were growing up. You still turned out okay. Or did you? You do your children a grave injustice when you shield them from the truth. Life can be hard and the tougher you are on them the better their chances of becoming successful. In the end, they will thank you for it. So, when your child comes to you wanting 15 different things for Christmas, give her a math lesson.

Sit her down. Show her your checkbook (hopefully it's accurate). Lay out all of the bills that need to be paid. Show her your check stub. And show her how long it will be before you get paid again. Not only will this exercise provide and excellent math lesson, but a sufficient reality check. Your child will walk away with a better understanding of personal finance and budgeting. And you will be surprised at how much she begins to pitch in and help around the house, once she realizes that mommy doesn't necessarily have a lot of money just because she ordered a new box of checks.

It's Better to Give

Let's continue with the topic at hand: why we shop.

Instead of calling yourself a shop-a-holic, it's better to consider yourself a giver, because your primary reason or motive for shopping should be to give to others unconditionally, not because you feel obligated. It should have a greater meaning than because you have to or because they bought you a gift. And don't give to make people think more highly of you. We already established the fact that you can't buy love (See Chapter 2). Instead, give as an outpour of love to others. Give for the joy and generosity of giving, no strings attached.

Another good reason/motive for giving is to fulfill a need. If someone is in need of something, the most considerate and functional gift you can give them would be one that fulfills his or her need. The recipient will greatly appreciate it and realize how much you truly care. It's not always easy. In fact, most times it requires a real sacrifice to give in this manner. However, when you give to fulfill someone's need you are acting as a minister of God. Remember, He supplies all our need.

If your friend is having car problems and she's worried about how she's going to get to and from work so she can make a living, purchasing her a box of scented candles from Target® won't make her problem go away. But giving her use of one of your two vehicles will make all the difference in the world. We know, because we've done it. Of course we know that giving a car away is a stretch for most people, but it would still be a very considerate gesture to give her a ride to work until she identifies a permanent solution.

In addition to giving purely for the joy of giving and giving to fulfill a need, our motive for shopping should be to challenge and encourage growth. A good example of shopping to challenge and encourage growth would be: You or maybe your friend desires a job promotion or perhaps wants to transition into another line of work. Well, in this case shopping for a new business suit to go on interviews would challenge and encourage you to apply for some positions. Similarly, buying a computer or purchasing and loading new software on your existing computer system would enhance your office skills and increase your earning potential. Items like these are functional as well as challenging and encouraging to your growth.

Always search for the purpose or motive behind your purchases before you reach the cashier counter and complete your sales transaction. If you cannot find a worthy reason for shopping, my advice to you is place that item right back on the shelf where you found it. It is crucial that you identify and adequately deal with what motivates you to shop.

Chapter 7 Exploratory Questions

1. Are spoiled rotten children an area of concern?
2. Will you take time to evaluate your motives before beginning holiday shopping?

Chapter Eight

How to Shop

Behold, I send you out as sheep in the midst of wolves. Therefore be wise as serpents... Matt. 10:16

Now that we have a handle on what our motivation for shopping should be, let's turn our attention to "how to shop." There are how to shop "do's" and how to shop "don'ts."

Do Diligence

A wise shopper makes educated shopping decisions, because he knows that well-informed decisions are usually good buying decisions. So how do we go about arming ourselves with information? Research is key. A shopper who is set on debt proofing the holidays does her homework. She takes the time to determine the true value and a fair price to pay for the goods or services she's in the market for.

Some of the avenues she might explore include: the internet (See Chapter 5), newspapers, magazines, television, radio ads and something many of us overlook, other people who have made similar purchases. So once she has performed a thorough investigation, she can buy with confidence that she received a great price. I might also add that some stores are so confident they offer the lowest prices, if you find the item advertised for less somewhere else, they will pay you the difference plus a certain percentage just to earn your business. This makes for a great deal.

Eating Up Your Savings

The next of our do's is one that most people overlook. That is, eating at home before/after going out to shop. Do I expect you not to take advantage of all the goodies especially the holiday treats that are available? You guessed it, woe is you! Spending money on fast food while shopping can really put a dent in your holiday budget. Let's face it, most shoppers commit several days to the task of holiday shopping. So, let's just say you spend 3 days shopping and you bring your two kids with you. You each consume 2 meals on each excursion, and you spend an average of $7 on each meal. That comes to a total of 18 meals and $126! Not to mention, some of us spend more than 3 days shopping for the holidays and it's quite easy to spend more than $7 on a meal.

So what if you don't have time to prepare a home cooked meal before shopping or if you are too tired to cook once you've finished shopping? Leftovers are always helpful at a time like this. Just pop them into the oven and VIOLA! You have a low cost meal that's probably healthier than fast food anyway. An alternative to combat mid shopping munchies is to bring your own snacks from home with you. Now you have covered all your bases and are armed and ready to shop.

Buy the Ton

Another one of the how to shop do's is: getting volume discounts. In other words, buying more than one of the same item for less than it would have been to purchase them separately. Say for instance the store offers a two for one sale. If you have a friend or a relative that has one of the same items on his list you can both benefit by getting a

50% discount just for shopping together.

Remember, this only works if the person you shop with is not a shop-a-holic. Your savings will go right down the drain if your shopping partner convinces you to buy other items that are not in your budget.

Likewise, you could also benefit from shopping with a partner if the store offers a discount when you buy a certain dollar amount worth of items. But once again you must be certain that you stay on course and are not unduly influenced by a shop-a-holic. Do you get the picture? We shouldn't buy just to get a discount, but if we can get a discount on something we plan to buy that's great. Remember, retailers offer discounts as an incentive to entice shoppers to buy more stuff- they are in the business of moving merchandise.

Undue Influence

In the Drama Free section of chapter five, we discussed emotional influences on our shopping endeavors. Here we are considering whether the influence another person may have on our shopping choices is good or bad. In other words, is it a good idea to have a shopping partner? You might wonder whether it helps to shop with someone else. Having someone to be a sounding board may keep you from impulse buying. It may be good to have a shopping partner, but it's not the more the merrier.

As a general rule, two is company but three is a crowd. The more people you invite to come along the better your chances of experiencing mass confusion. Also, if you choose a shopping partner, pick someone who is more frugal and practical than you. Their discipline might rub off on you and help you stay within your budget. But bare in mind, as I have already alluded to, it's better to shop alone than to have a shop-a-holic tag along with you. Not all company is good company and not all influence is a positive influence.

Paper or Plastic

Let's begin the how to shop don'ts with avoiding credit card spending. Unless you have created your budget and you know you will be able to pay the bill in full, experts suggest that you just say no to charging. And I agree whole-heartedly. As mentioned earlier, high interest rates may cause you to end up paying four times the price of the item purchased. You may wonder whether borrowing from relatives or close friends is a sound alternative to credit card spending. Unfortunately, this is still a form of debt. In our first book "Got MONEY?" we talk about the dangers of borrowing money. And let's not forget the mission is to debt proof the holidays.

An Offer You Can Refuse

The next how to shop don't is don't fall for store card offers. There are many tricks of the trade, and the debt proof shopper must beware! Some of the more popular tricks include:

1. The no payments for a specified period of time sham
2. The no interest for a certain time frame scam
3. The 10% off when you open a new account today scheme.

In the above cases you are being enticed to buy items you probably otherwise could not afford or would not have bought in the first place. Also, the prices have been marked up sufficiently to compensate for the so called bargain they claim they are giving you.

And let's not forget that the interest rate on store cards is usually even higher than the traditional credit cards (i.e., Mastercard®, Visa®, American Express® and Discover®). Our goal is no debt not more debt!

Take Your Pulse

The final how to shop don't is avoid impulse buying. It's sad but true; many people get in trouble on this one alone. So consider yourselves warned. We learned in chapter four that merchandising is a multi-trillion dollar industry (U.S. Commerce Department statistics). Don't think that where goods are located in a store is a haphazard accident determined by some teen-age sales person as part of their after-school job. Highly paid experts have done extensive research and have concluded where various types of products are to be placed to maximize sales.[5] As a result product manufactures/distributors are often willing to pay a premium to have their goods strategically located to obtain the maximum exposure and highest potential for consumer purchases.

Don't fall prey to this tactic. All that glitters isn't gold. Don't be moved by finely crafted product placements. Stick to your game plan. Before purchasing you must ask yourself do I need it and

---

[5] See About.com for glossary of definitions and additional information on: visual merchandising, planogramming and space management software and systems.

do I need it now. If the answer to both these questions isn't yes, back away from the counter with your hands up! I promise you will be glad you did. In other words, if it's not on your gift list (See Chapter 1) and you haven't done your homework on the price (See the beginning of this chapter), don't buy it.

Chapter 8 Exploratory Questions

1. How much time is spent researching to ensure a fair price is obtained on purchases?
2. Is dining out while shopping eating up your savings?
3. Is shopping with a shop-a-holic defeating the purpose of seeking volume discounts?
4. Would it be better to shop alone?
5. Is the temptation to use credit cards to finance holiday spending overwhelming?
6. Has using no payments, no interest or new card offers ever backfired?
7. Are impulsive holiday purchases causing an unnecessary financial burden?

Chapter Nine

Gifts That Keep On Giving

For God so loved the world that He gave His only begotten Son, that whoever believes in Him should not perish but have everlasting life. John 3:16

We closed the last chapter revisiting our gift list concept, so let's discuss the types of gifts we plan on buying. Is it just me or does it seem that many of the gifts that are given today fall quite short of fulfilling the reasons why we should give that we discussed earlier in the "Why Shop" chapter? The average gifts have been done over and over again with little if any thought given in many cases.

Eternally Yours

The people at the top of our shopping lists generally are parents and children if we have any. Exactly how many more ties do you think dad can stomach? Or how many more bottles of perfume can mom fit on her dresser? In either case, the answer is probably not many. The thrill has long since been gone away. They probably don't even remember who gave them what tie or what perfume anymore. Speaking of the thrill being gone, what about the kids? They outgrow the clothes before you can blink, and those overpriced toys end up at the bottom of the heap within weeks (if not sooner). How many more dolls and video games do they need? If you haven't seen Toy Story Two®, rent it. By the way, neither dolls nor video games seem to foster much creativity.

When I was young we played board games. They fostered creativity, and they didn't cost much either. They were also educational. I often explain how Monopoly® made me a businessman, as it taught me the basics about money management, negotiating, purchasing property, mortgages and collecting rental income. I learned these valuable lessons while enjoying hours of entertainment and

quality time with family members and friends.
So let's share some of the alternative gifts that keep
on giving. In addition to board games, CD's,
books, DVD's and audio tapes make for great gifts.
They often have a lasting impact like Monopoly®
did for me. The great thing is these are not just
good gifts for children. Adults enjoy them too.
Some of my favorite gifts have been CD's. I might
add that they make great alternatives to sitting in
front of the television.

These gifts should also be tailored to the particular
interest of the recipient. This ensures they will
provide hours of entertainment, and it shows you
cared enough to personalize the gift.

Money is a universal gift that keeps on giving.
Although I know a lot of people who don't mind
that gift, I'm not suggesting that you give cash. I
meant giving gifts in the form of investments like:
savings bonds or shares of stock. My wife and I
started this tradition with our God-children several
years ago. It works out really well, because in
addition to reaping a future financial benefit it's
educational. And it's never too early to start
teaching youth the value of a dollar.

Our Godchildren love it when we tell them how the
government bonds we bought them will be worth
twice what we paid for them in ten years. And
stocks have averaged a return of about 10% per year
over the last 75 years! And both stocks and bonds

may have beneficial tax advantages. As you can
see, there are many alternate gifts that keep giving.

Chapter 9 Exploratory Questions

1. Can you see any future value in the gifts that you
traditionally have given?

Epilogue

We've addressed the what, where, when, why and how of debt proof shopping and gifts that keep on giving. We offer proven safety measures. Just as homes are child-proofed so that young children don't injure themselves playing, you should debt-proof your holidays so that you don't injure yourself shopping.

Remember the Reason for the Season

We would like to reiterate, Christmas is a holy day, not just another holiday. Jesus is the reason for the season. We should share our blessings with our local churches, as well as, those less fortunate. There are many places where Christians and others enslaved. We should lend our support and prayers. Below is a list of some of the organizations are being persecuted and in some cases even committed to helping those less fortunate throughout the world.

1. Save Africa's Children
   www.saveafricaschildren.com
2. Save Darfur Coalition www.savedarfur.org
3. Bridge of Hope www.rodparsley.com/boh
4. Life Today www.lifetoday.org
5. Feed the Children www.feedthechildren.org

Congratulations. By taking the time to read this book, you have made a sound investment that will surely reap great rewards. We sincerely pray that our words have in some way inspired you. If you have been blessed by Debt Proofing Your Holidays, by all means recommend it to a friend. After all, we are blessed to be a blessing.

Much of the information you've read and more will be available in our upcoming book, Debt Proof Shopping (working title). Debt Proof Shopping will include car buying, home buying, paying for college and other money saving, debt proof tips.

Debt Proof Shopping will be available for sale on our website along with our books in the Escape From Debtors Prison series: *Got Money?*, *Let My People Go!* and *Debt Proofing Your Holidays*.

Well, that about wraps it up. No pun intended.

Epilogue

May your holidays be joyous and debt proof!

For a list of our other products, log on to our website. www.pottsinternational.com
For mail-in orders, our address is Post Office Box 13921, Torrance, CA 90503.

If you have any questions or comments, or would like to take our debt free message to your church, community group or investment club, call or email us.

Our telephone number is (818) 501-1358.

E-mail address: hisfavor@aol.com

Have a very Merry Christmas and a Happy Holiday Season.

May God richly bless you.

Suggested Resources

Potts, Rachelle and Tyrone, *Escape From Debtors Prison:*
Got Money?, Torrance, CA 90503, El Shaddai Publishing, 2000. (818) 501-1358

Potts, Rachelle and Tyrone, *Escape From Debtors Prison:*
Let My People Go!, Torrance, CA 90503, El Shaddai Publishing, 2001. (818) 501-1358

Helpful Websites

www.DebtFreeChristian.org
www.ChristianDebt.org
www.ebay.com
www.priceline.com
www.amazon.com
www.merchantfraudsquad.com
www.about.com
www.smartmoney.com
www.money.com
www.quicken.com
www.fool.com
www.cardweb.com
www.debtorsanonymous.org

Credit Counselors

Trinity Financial (800) 646-6146
Debt Free Christian (800) 624-9747
Consumer Credit Counseling Service
(800) 388-CCCS
Debtors Anonymous (212) 624-8220

Credit Bureaus

Experian (888) 397-3742
Equifax (800) 685-1111
TransUnion (800) 888-4213

About the Authors

Minister Tyrone Potts has been a *'business man'* more than twenty-five years. Though born to a large family of modest means, Tyrone envisioned more. He opened his first bank account at age six, then his entrepreneurial spirit soared. Tyrone established his first profitable business at eight-years-old. At age twelve, he began investing. After obtaining a degree in Business Administration from Georgetown University, Tyrone became a Certified Public Accountant and worked for one of the top five accounting firms in the world. More than seventeen years of experience in both public and private accounting credits his expertise in business and accounting.

Rachelle Potts is a licensed Evangelist Missionary. She obtained a social science degree from Dillard University and attended Loyola University School of Law. Rachelle's prior career experience include mediator for the Los Angeles County Bar Association and arbitrator for the Council of Better Business Bureaus. She specialized in resolving business and finance related conflicts. Rachelle has reconciled the discrepancies of corporate clients in the banking industry. Also, formerly employed as both a stockbroker and a fund-raiser, she's spent her career working for financial institutions and undertaking fiscal affairs at non-profits.

The Potts are anointed for their assignment to economically empower people. Their financial backgrounds and professional experiences contribute to their mastery of money, uniquely qualifying them to revolutionize the way we view our resources. The Potts teach from first-hand experience. They also practice what they preach: eliminating nearly $100,000 of debt in three years on mainly one income. They released the first three books of the Escape From Debtors Prison series, *Got Money?*, *Let My People Go! and Debt Proofing Your Holidays*. *Debt Proof Shopping, Rise Up & Possess* and *Romance & Finance* are other books in the series that will be released in coming years.

Prosperity Outpouring To The Saints, Intl.
Post Office Box 13921 Torrance, CA 90503
(818) 501-1358 email: hisfavor@aol.com
www.pottsinternational.com

After product description, please list quantity next
to unit price.

Family Budget & Debt Priority Payoff Plan
24.99

Software that helps you manage your money and
get out of debt.

Get Out Of Debt Presentation Packet
39.99

A hard copy of the information taught in the
seminar and CD's.

Powerful Principles of Prosperity
14.99

Framed 5'7" plaque of the 10 commandments for
success.

Escape From Debtors Prison: Got MONEY?
14.99

Book on 8 methods of obtaining money.

Escape From Debtors Prison: Let My People Go!
14.99

Book on getting out and staying out of debt.

**Escape From Debtors Prison: Debt Proofing
Your Holidays   7.99**

Book on honoring Jesus while enjoying Christmas
and not overspending.

30 minute Audio CD   7.00

The Spirit of Compromise: What's Standing
Between You and God's Best

Shipping & Handling $3.95 per unit

Subtotal   _____

* Optional....Love gifts and offerings are also
appreciated. (not tax deductible)   _____

TOTAL   _____

Name_____
Address_____
City_____State___Zip_____

___Yes include me on your emailing list for
seminars, products and prayer.